Shadow and Sunshine

ELIZA SUGGS.

SHADOW AND SUNSHINE

BY

ELIZA SUGGS

———— ————

Thou art my hiding place; thou shalt preserve me from trouble; thou shalt compass me about with songs of deliverance.—*Selah, Ps. 23:7.*

————————

OMAHA, NEB.
1906.

Copyright 1906,

by Eliza Suggs.

Introduction.

While attending a camp meeting near Alma, Nebraska, during the summer of 1895, my attention was drawn to a little colored girl sitting in a baby cab, who appeared to take a deep interest in the services. I was told that it was Sister Eliza Suggs, who, amid deep affliction, was developing into a strong Christian character.

While the reader will be touched by the scenes of suffering related in this narrative, he will be impressed that Eliza does not belong to the despondent class. She is evidently of a cheerful temperament, possessing an overcoming faith which gives her the assurance that the God whom she loves and serves, intends to provide for and sustain her until life's journey is ended. She saw light where others would have seen only darkness; she cherished hope where others would have felt only despair; and fearing it might displease her Master, she rejected offers of worldly gain which others would have eagerly grasped. Of humble parentage, limited advantages, physical embarassments, she is shedding rays of light along her pathway, and making impressions for good on the hearts and lives of those with whom she associates. What a marvel of grace!

It is not strange that one into whose life a kind Providence has brought so much of comfort, amid suffering; so much the world her life story. I believe much amid privation, should desire to give to of joy, amid sorrow; so much of blessing good will be accomplished by the circulation of this simple narrative, written, as I believe it to have been, purely for the glory of God. It will serve to forcibly illustrate how one in sore affliction and deep privation may possess the grace of perfect resignation to the will of God, and be ready for any service he may require.

BURTON R. JONES.

Personal Reminiscences and Testimony.

C. M. DAMON.

With much pleasure I learn that Sister Eliza Suggs, colored, of Orleans, Neb., is to bring out a book or biography and reminiscences of her parents. I know nothing in detail of her plans, but I shall be surprised if the book is not one of thrilling interest. The author is a most remarkable young woman. Born of such heritage of physical infirmity as is seldom known, she has surmounted incredible difficulties and made progress in education, light labor, and the development of Christian character, that is the astonishment and admiration of her multitude of friends. She is a mite of body— apparently less than the upper third of a normal growth.

Carried in arms or wheeled about in a carriage, her frail hands and well developed head have accomplished wonders, obtaining a fair education, which makes her a valuable assistant, sometimes as secretary of religious organizations and work. In former years she assisted her father, more or less, in evangelistic work, and she has presided in public meetings with marked dignity and ability. Carried on the plaform and moved about as occasion required by kind and willing attendants, I have perhaps never seen more clock-like precision than the execution of an interesting program, at which she presided in a public temperance meeting in the M. E. Church, during my last pastorate in Orleans.

She is one of several sons and daughters of most estimable Christian parents, who were born in slavery, whose thrilling story will be told in the book of which this may form a brief chapter. Her father was one of the ablest and comeliest preachers of his race whom I have known. He considered himself of unmixed blood. His manly form, fine countenance, and strong and melodious voice, made him attractive, both in speech and song.

When the author of this book was very young, I was witness of a most exciting episode in his remarkable history. We were on a camp ground in western Kansas. On Sabbath morning the service had closed and many had retired from the Tabernacle. Bro. Suggs had not yet left the platform where he had been speaking. He was tappped on the shoulder and requested to step outside when three men quickly handcuffed him and rushed him from the grounds. I was instantly notified that he had called for me and Rev. E. E. Miller. I reached him about forty rods away as they were ready to drive off the ground. He held up his manacled hands and with unaffected indignation, exclaimed: James Suggs, *a murderer!*" I inquired the meaning, and was informed he was a suspect from Ohio for whom a large reward was offered. The fearful blunder of a bungling detective and his assistants was apparent; but that did not help in the excitement of the moment. I assured them of the error, asked what word I should send his wife; was requested to look after his horse tied on the ground, and they were gone. While others sought his release by legal means, unavailing, as he was so swiftly driven from one county to another, I telegraphed a friend in Topeka to see the Governor, and have the Ohio requisition refused, if it should be presented, as seemed probable. I then wrote Ex-governor St. John, who had employed him and the refugees which had poured into Kansas during the

noted exodus from the South, and informed his old neighbors of Princeton, Ill. All
this proved unnecessary, for in a day or
two he was taken before a Justice in Osborne county, and speedily demonstrated
their mistake. The false arrest cost the
detective severely, and it would have gone
harder with him but for an error in the
accusation under which he was confined
for some time and brought to trial. An
account of this singular affair may be
detailed elsewhere. My efforts, occasion-
ed by the excitement of the hour, served
to bring out varied testimonials to his
worth and high esteem in which he was
held.

Bro. Suggs has long since joined the
throng of the ransomed ones, while his
companion remains an honored and be-
loved pilgrim among the saints of Orleans.

One other thought comes to mind in
this connection—his realization and en-

joyment of what he sang so beautifully, the first time I ever heard it, "The Toils of the Road will seem Nothing when I get to the End of the Way."

The devotion to the author of her sister, Katie, for years a member of the Official Board at Orleans, is something interesting and touching. Hard working as she is at home and away, she seems never to tire of the care of her afflicted but honored charge. When Eliza, hidden in church behind the seats in front, would testify, Kate rises with her in arms, and she speaks clearly and forcibly. There is not a family among our people in the place more respected or more deservedly so. Boarding with them for eight months, with every care and kindness shown, the writer witnesses that he never saw an improper act or heard an improper word. Having heard from the lips of Sister Suggs many an incident of slave days and war times, I shall await with interest the appearance of the forthcoming book.

Sketch of Father.

'Some suck up poison from a sorrow's core,
  As naught but nightshade grew upon earth's
      ground;
Love turned all his to heart'sease, and the more
Fate tried his bastions, she but forced a door,
  Leading to sweeter manhood and more sound."
                    —James Russell Lowell.

My father and mother were slaves.
Father was born in North Carolina, August 15th, 1831. He was a twin, and was
sold away from his parents and twin
brother, Harry, at the age of three years.
This separation, at so tender an age, was
for all time, as never again did he see
his loved ones. In after years he had a
faint recollection of his mother, and
could remember distinctly the words of
introduction with which he was handed
over from his old master to his new:
"Whip that boy and make him mind."

A slave had no real name of his own, but was called by the name of his master; and whenever he was sold and changed masters, his name was changed to that of the new master. The parents gave his first, or Christian name, however, which was usually retained amid all his changing of masters. Father's parents named him James. So at this time his name was James Martin. He was sold by Mr. Martin for a hundred dollars, and taken to Mississippi. Afterward he was sold to Jack Kindrick, and again to Mr. Suggs, with whom he remained until the war broke out.

Father was a blacksmith by trade, and was considered a valuable slave. Mr. Suggs was a kind master, and as James was an industrious and obedient servant, he was allowed the privilege, ·after his day's work was done, of working after night for himself. He made pancake griddles, shovels, tongs, and other small

articles, the proceeds from the sale of
which brought in many a small coin. He
was also allowed, in odd moments, to cul-
tivate a small garden patch, on his own
responsibility, and it was surprising
what that little patch was made to yield.
Naturally proud and ambitious, the
money thus obtained was usually spent
upon his person, enabling him to dress
better and appear to much better advantage than his less enterprising compeers.

Slaves were not allowed to have an education. Father said he had to "pick
up" what education he got, much as a
rabbit might be supposed to pick up some
tender morsel with the greyhounds hot in
pursuit. When the master's children came
from school, they would make letters and
say, "Jim, you can't make that." But
he would make it and find out what it
was. Again he would say to them, "You
can't spell "horse, "or "dog," or some
other word he wanted to know. And they

would reply, "Yes, I can," and would spell it. All this time he was learning, while they had no idea that he was storing these things up in his mind. Yes, he had to steal what learning he got.

While James was still quite young, Mr. Suggs bought a little slave girl, named Malinda Filbrick. In time, Jame and Malinda came to love each other, and were married while yet in their teens. The same pride of heart which had manifested itself in his own stylish appearance, now prompted him to lavish his extra earnings on his young bride. One instance of his extravagant indulgence was the purchase of a $7.00 pair of ear-drops, which doubtless afforded him much gratification until the ill-fated day when they proved too strong a temptation to a party of Union soldiers, who carried them off as spoils. Another outlay of his surplus earnings was in the purchase, for his wife, of a remarkable quilt, made after

Mrs. Malinda Suggs.

the pattern known as "the chariot-wheel."
This was truly a masterpiece of skill, and
was highly prized by my mother.   It
seemed about to share the same fate as
the ear-drops and was in the hands of a
Union soldier, when the earnest plead-
ings of my mother prevailed upon the
kind-hearted officer in charge to give or-
ders for its restoration.

While still in slavery, father was won-
derfully converted. Before his conversion
he was a wicked young man. Pride in
dress was not his only besetment. He
loved to danc and drink, and have as
good a time, from a worldly standpoint,
as any human being could who was held
in bondage. Whenever a slave wanted
to go out to spend the evening he had to
get a pass from his master; for there
were more men called patrolment, elected
according to law, whose duty it was to
seize and thoroughly chastise any slave
who was so presumptious as to venture

out without a pass. If a slave was caught
out after nine o'clock at night, without a
pass, he was stripped to the waist and
beaten thirty lashes on his naked back.
It was against the law to whip a slave
over his clothing. One night these patrolment caught father out without a
pass. He well knew what was to follow,
and as they held him by the coat collar,
he straightened back his arms and ran
out of the coat leaving it in their hands.
They got the coat, but James never got
the whipping.

After he was converted, he would go
to his master and ask to be allowed to go
to meeting, and permission having been
given, he would say, "And please, sir,
may I have a pass?" At these meetings
he would talk and exhort his fellow-
slaves, until Mr. Suggs would say, "If
James keeps on like this, he will surely
make a preacher."

Father loved freedom; or at least he thought he should enjoy it. He never had been a free man, and hardly knew how it would seem to be free. But it is natural to every man, of whatever race or color, to want to be free. He used often to say to his young wife, "When the car of freedom comes along, I am going to get on board;" meaning that if he got a chance he was going to the war.

One day the news came that the "Yankees" were within four miles of Ripley, the village near which Mr. Suggs lived. They were reported as having a heavy force of both calvary and infantry. Mr. Suggs was a very wealthy man and had a large number of fine horses and carriages, as well as great herds of cattle and sheep. All these he must hide, as best he could, from the "Yankees," for they were very destructive to the property of the southerners. So he called his men to gather up his belongings, as far as possible, and take them to the cane-brake to hide them. The canes grow so thickly together, and the leaves so interwoven, as to make it impossible to see any object at a distance of even a few feet. So a cane-brake was a fine place for hiding.

Mr. Suggs called James and told him to take his sheep and go at once to the cane-brake, which he did. Little did my mother think, as she saw him go, that this would be the last she would see of James for three years and nine months. But so it was to be. When the "Yankees" came, a colored man took them and showed them where these treasures were hidden, together with the belongings of several neighbors. The soldiers helped themselves to whatever they wanted; and told the slaves that any who wanted to do so might go with them. Father thought his time had come to strike for liberty. He went into the war and fought for his freedom and that of his family, and obtained it as a well-earned victory.

Many of the slaves, in making their escape north with the Union army, took with them their wives and children. So father fondly hoped he could get some soldiers to come back with him to get mother and the four children. He knew but little of army life and discipline, and so was bitterly disappointed in never getting back.

When the excitement was over and the soldiers gone, and some of the slaves came back to the plantation, father did not appear. Mr. Suggs came to mother and said, " Malinda, where is James?" "I don't know," said mother. "Didn't you send him off with the sheep?" But he would not believe her when she said she didn't know. He blamed her for father's going away, and thought she had put him up to go.

Father enlisted in 1864, but was wounded shortly after and discharged from active service and sent to the hospital. After recovering from his wound, he joined the regular service and continued until the close of the war, part of the time acting as corporal of his company. When the war was over, he came north with his captain, Mr. Newton. The thought uppermost in his mind, was how to get his family from the south. For him to have gone after them, in person, at that time, would have been at the risk of his life. Mr. Newton, having business in the south, and being a kind-hearted man, father begged of him to go and find his family and bring them to him. This Captain Newton did, finding them not far from where father had left them.

Father now went to work with great zeal at his trade to earn money for the purpose of getting a home for his family. He was at last a *free* man, with his dear family —a *free* family, and living in his own *free* country. The slaves could not be married as white people were; for there was a clause in the marriage ceremony which gave the slave-holder the right to separate husband and wife whenever he chose to do so. I have heard my mother say that she has known instances where husband and wife have been separated after having been married only a few weeks, or even only a few days. My father said that seeing he was now a free man, he wanted to be married like other free people. So on the fifth day of June, in 1866, father and mother were married again according to the Christian rites, or according to the white man's law.

Father continued to work at his trade until God called him to preach the Gospel. He had a great struggle over his call to preach. He had worldly ambitions and was making money, and it was hard for him to give up all and follow Christ. Finally he consented to preach, but did not go at it with his whole heart. He would preach occasionally, but still worked at his blacksmithing, until one night the Lord spoke to him plainly. He said it was like an audible voice saying, "Either preach the Gospel or work at your trade." He was to make his choice, but it meant to him heaven or hell. Which would he take? He trembled as he felt the responsibility of leading lost souls to Christ. But he made his choice and said, "Yes," to God. He began preaching around in school houses. Large crowds gathered to hear him, and from that time on, it was the business of his life to minister Divine truth to dying men and women.

In 1874 he was given exhorter's license, by Rev. C. E. Harroun, Jr., in the Illinois Conference of the Free Methodist church. In 1878 he was given a local preacher's license by Rev. Edwin C. Best, pastor of the Sheffield circuit, Galva district, of the Illinois Conference. In 1879 he was ordained deacon in the Illinois

Conference, by General Superintendent
B. T. Roberts, and in 1884, in the West
Kansas Conference, he was ordained el-
der by General Superintendent E. P.
Hart.

His labors during the early years of his
ministry were in the Illinois Conference.
Rev. C. W. Sherman came to Princeton,
where we lived, with a band of workers
and held a tent meeting. This band con-
sisted of C. L. Lamberts and wife, F. D.
Brooke, and Lizzie Bardell, now his wife;
D. M. Smashey, and Belle Christie, now
his wife. These band workers have since
developed into prominent preachers and
evangelists in the Free Methodist church,
some of them having filled the office of district elder for several years. They were
at this time entertained in our home.
While the meeting was in progress one
night the rowdies gathered, cut down the
large tabernacle and threw stones into
the small tents. Brother Sherman tried

to persuade them to desist when one
struck him in the eye, nearly putting out
his eye. Brother Smashey received a cut
in his head, from which pools of blood
stood around the tent.

Next morning my father looked down
toward the camp ground and saw that the
tent was down, and he and mother went
down with sorrowful hearts to comfort
the workers. Brother Sherman met them
with a joyful, "Praise the Lord, Sister
Suggs, I shall preach tonight if I haven't
either eye." And he did, with a bandage
around his eye. And with another bandage around Brother Smashey's head, they
looked like soldiers after a battle. The
Lord gave a grand victory, for the hearts
of the people were turned toward them in
sympathy. A good collection was taken
to defray the expenses of the meeting, the
tent was raised, and the meeting went on
with power. Souls were saved and added
to the small society already organized in

that place. The city authorities promised protection from future disturbance, and kept their promise.

In the year 1879 father went to Kansas as an evangelist. This was the year of the great drouth and grasshopper scourge. There was a colony of colored people, who had come from the south and settled in Graham county, Kansas, naming their little settlement Nicodemus. Father went to preach to these people. He found them in a suffering condition, nearly starving, and with scarcely enough clothing to cover their nakedness. Father visited Hon. John P. St. John, at that time Governor of Kansas, to see what could be done for these people. The governor sent him back to Illinois to solicit aid for them; for, said he, "After you have provided for their temporal needs, then they can hear your Gospel." He solicited accordingly in Illinois, and sent back barrel after barrel of clothing to the people.

He afterward took up a homestead in Phillips county, Kansas, and in the year 1885 brought his family to Kansas. He was now almost constantly in the work of the Lord. He often said, "I would sooner wear out than rust out," and surely God granted him the desire of his heart.

But while he was thus working earnestly to build up God's kingdom, Satan was just as busily at work to hinder and destroy his labors. Jesus said to Simon Peter, "Simon, Simon, behold Satan hath desired to have you, that he may sift you as wheat; but I have prayed for thee." Ah! here was Peter's only strength, "I have prayed for thee." In the power of those prayers, and in that alone, could he overcome. The same old enemy is in the world today and his hatred and spite toward God's children is just as strong as it was in Peter's day. He still desires to have God's little ones that he may sift them as wheat.

The powers of darkness were now turned loose upon father. Wicked men laid
hands upon him and took him to prison.
This occurred on the camp ground at Mar-
vin, Kansas. One afternoon, after he was
through preaching, some one came up to
him and said, "Brother Suggs, some one
wants to see you." He was led out supposing he was going to have a talk with
some old friend or with some one who was
inquiring the way to God, as many such
came to him for counsel. He found himself being handcuffed and being hurried
away between two disguised detectives,
who accused him of being one Harrison
Page, an escaped murderer. In vain he
pleaded innocence. "You are Harrison
Page," said his accusers. "Your name is
not James Suggs. You are a murderer."
Imagine his surprise! But the Lord blessed him right there, and as he was led
away, he was heard praising the Lord.
The last word he said to the brethren was,

"Take good care of old Dollie, and see that she has plenty of water, take her home, and tell wife I will come out all right." One looking on observed, "Any man in such a condition as that, arrested and accused of murder, taking thought of an old horse like Dolly, surely can't be a very bad man, Suggs is innocent." Rev. C. M. Damon was tireless in his efforts for father's release, and with characteristic foresight, telegraphed a friend in Topeka to see the Governor, and wrote to ex-Governor John P. St. John and to father's old neighbors in Princeton, Illinois. Rev. E. E. Miller, now in heaven, pursued after the captors, the brethren made up money to pay his expenses and kept him right after them, until father was proven innocent and set free.

Doubtless it was the intention and expectation of the enemy, in making this bold accusation, to silence father forever from preaching. But in this he overshot

the mark. Father never ceased preaching
on this account; but on the other hand, it
gave him new opportunities for preaching
the Gospel. Even in jail he held meetings,
and one man who heard him was converted and called to preach. Father lived
convictions on his accusers. He talked
to them about their souls and their hard
hearts melted. They knew he was innocent, and really wanted to get rid of him
before they could do so. His accusers
were afterward arrested and brought to
trial. After father was cleared and re-
leased, and while waiting for his accusers'
trial, he started a meeting in Osborne,
Kansas. Thus God caused the wrath of
man to praise him, and opened new and
unexpected doors for the spread of the
Gospel.

This arrest and seizure of father, and
the suspense which followed, were a
strange and hard ordeal for the family at
home. My mother has been through the

fire, but the same God who was with her in slavery days was with her at this time. Father was mercifully restored to his family, all safe and sound, and went on his way rejoicing. Doors of usefulness were opened to him on every side. He was quite widely known within the bounds of several different conferences, the Illinois, Iowa, West Iowa, Kansas, West Kansas, and Nebraska conferences, each having claimed some share of his time and labor.

Attracted by the Free Methodist Seminary at Orleans, Nebraska, and desiring for his daughters the advantages it afforded, he moved his family thither in 1886. But he did not settle down or superannuate because he had moved to a community that was well supplied with preachers and Christian workers. It was only for convenience and the welfare of his family that he was led to take this step, and not with any intention of dropping out of the Lord's work. From this as a center, he

REV. JAMES SUGGS

went out to different places for evangel-
stic labors, and kept the revival fire burn-
ing brightly in his own heart through the
heat of summer as well as through the
cold of winter.

The last winter he was on earth, being
the winter of 1888-89, he was engaged in
a protracted campaign against sin, on the
Sappa Creek, in Norton County, Kansas.
He pitched his tabernacle on the farm of
'Father Neimyer," and here once more set
the battle in array. He banked up the
tabernacle on the outside, and put in it
two stoves, which made it very comfort-
ible. The attendance and interest were
good, and souls were born into the kingdom of God. After closing this series of
meetings in the tabernacle, he held others
in the neighboring schoolhouses, and thus
put in the winter solidly for God. It was
the privilege of my mother and myself to
be with him in all these meetings. How

little we realized that these were his last
on earth!

He returned home from his winter's
campaign, weary and exhausted. He de-
cided to rest a little and be ready to go
again. After resting a few weeks he went
on an evangelistic tour east, but soon returned home again sick, and took his bed.
His disease baffled all the skill of the
physicians, and after an illness of
about five weeks during which he manifested great patience and resignation, on
the 22nd of May, 1889, he passed peace-
fully home to God. His funeral at Orleans
was largely attended, not only by his
brethren and sisters in the church, but
by the citizens of Orleans who thus showed their appreciation and respect.

But none knew his worth so well as
his own family. He was the strong staff
upon which mother and all of us had
leaned. How should we ever learn to walk
alone? "Leaning on the Everlasting

Arms," we have since learned to mount up on wings as eagles over all our difficulties, to run the Christian race and not grow weary, and to walk with the Lord and not faint. Father, we miss thee—as much now as ever we did—yet would not recall thee. Rest, weary soldier, rest from thy labors! Thy works shall follow thee. Thy reward shall be sure. A part, at least of your family is travelling the road our father trod. We have caught the spirit of your loved battle song, and sing with you,

"We'll end this warfare,
    Down by the river;
We'll end this warfare
    Down by the riverside."

By and by God shall say to each one of us, as he said to you, "It is enough; come up higher."

"And when the battle's over
We shall wear a crown
    In the New Jerusalem."

And then, when the last battle has been fought, and the last victory has been won, and the last enemy has been destroyed, then and not till then, shall we lay our armor down, and through all eternity,

"We will walk through the streets of the
        city
With our loved ones gone before;
We will stand on the banks of the river,
We will meet them there to part no
        more."

Sketch of Mother.

"When we are sick, where can we turn for succor?
When we are wretched, where can we complain?
And when the world looks cold and surly on us,
Where can we go to meet a warmer eye
With such sure confidence as to a mother?"
—Selected.

My mother was born in Alabama, April 5th, 1834, and when quite young went with her parents to Mississippi. Her mother was a slave belonging to a Mr McArthur. He had several sons and when he died his slaves were divided among his sons. In the division, parents and children were separated from each other, and thus mother was separated from her mother and eight brothers, but not far. She could go and see them occasionally. My mother was never ill-treated like some of the slaves were, but my poor grandmother was.

One night while the old man, McArthur, was still living, he and one of his sons went to town. They were both in the habit of drinking. So on this particular night they got drunk and gambled away their money and came home in a rage. Grandmother had to sit up late to keep their supper warm. She was afraid to go to bed, but finally dropped to sleep and the fire died down. Sometime in the small hours of the night, they came home. With a start she awoke, and tried to fix the fire. But as she stooped to stir the fire in the fire-place, the old man kicked her in the eye and put it out. But this was not punishment enough. Early the next morning he called her out to be whipped. What was all this for? What was all this for? What had she done? He accused her of stealing his money! So she was stripped to the waist and beaten on her naked back until it was raw like beef, and as he threw the whips with which he had beaten her on the ground, the dogs licked the blood from them. But grandmother must continue to go to the field and work, notwithstanding her raw back and consequent high fever.

My mother was a little girl then, and while grandmother was being beaten and was crying so, the little girl would scream and pretend to be sick, thinking the master would surely let her mother go to come to her sick child. But no! He paid no attention to her screams. After the old man McArthur died, my mother was taken by one of the sons. But he being a hard drinker, got into debt and my mother had to be sold.

A Mr. Fillbrick now bought her. Mrs. Fillbrick was a good Christian woman, and took a great deal of interest in her little slave girl. She taught her to read and was always kind to her. She would sometimes talk out her heart to mother, young as she was, perhaps for want of

any one else to talk to.   At such times
she would tell her that it was very wrong
to keep slaves; but as she was not strong
enough to do her own work, and had to
have help, of course it was necessary for
her to buy one.   Mother was the only ser-
in her house and necessarily had much
work to do.

Mrs. Fillbrick, although so kind and
gentle in disposition, was not very well
liked among her neighbors and mother
often wondered why.   But after she was
older she knew the reason.   It was because Mrs. Fillbrick opposed slavery.
Speaking almost prophetically, she would
sometimes tell mother that some day the
slaves would all be free. Soon this woman
left the south, and of course, had to sell
her slave.

Mr. Suggs, my father's master, now
bought her, and thus my father and mother were brought together for the first
time.   After they were married they were

never torn from each other and sold to
different masters; for Mr. Suggs said he
did not believe in separating husband and
wife.   Thus God dealt very tenderly with
my parents and spared them the horrors
and heartaches which were the common
lot of most slaves.

Under this comparatively kind and in-
dulgent master, my mother knew little
of real trouble.   Her first experiences
that might be called real troubles came
after my father had gone to the war. Mr.
Suggs, fearing that my father would come
back and get mother and her four children, took the two older children, Ellen
and Franklin, to Georgia.   I will say
here, that when the Union soldiers were
around the slaves could just walk off before their master's eyes, and he dare not
say a word.   So by separating the family, Mr. Suggs seemed more likely to prevent their escape with the Union soldiers.
When Ellen and Frank were sent away,

Lucinda, the next little girl, would have been taken too, but she was sick at the time. So she and baby Calvin were left with their mother. And now followed dark days for mother. Husband gone, she knew not where, and herself blamed for his escape; and now her two children in strange hands and carried away to a strange land! She had also a sister belonging to the same master. To add to her troubles, her sister died at this time. It seemed her cup of bitterness was more than full.

Baby Calvin was very cross. Mother had no time to care for him properly, as she was the only woman servant on the place and had ten cows to milk and all the cooking to do. So her little children were neglected, for this work *must* be done. One day Calvin was sitting on the kitchen floor crying loudly, and mother had no time to take him. The mistress came in, and hearing the baby crying, she

chugged his head up against the brick
wall. How he did scream! Mother said,
"You had better kill him and be done with
it." The mistress angrily replied, "Let
the nasty stinking little rascal behave
himself, then; he is a chip off from the old
block," meaning he was too much like his
father.

Mother was professing religion before
father went away, but was ignorant of
the way of real salvation; and instead of
her troubles driving her nearer the Lord,
she wandered further and further away,
and at last ceased praying altogether. Her
troubles preyed upon her mind so that she
lost her appetite and could not sleep. She
grew weaker and weaker until she could
no longer get through with her work.
Finally she came to herself. She thought,
"I must not die, but must live for the
sake of my two little ones. She began
calling on the Lord for help, wept her way
back to the cross, and was restored to the

Divine favor. There came to her new strength and courage to meet life's battles. She inquired of the Lord as to whether she should ever again see her husband and children. Clearly and definitely came the answer, "You shall see them again." She began trusting in the Lord, and was touched and helped in her body.

As to any direct word from her husband, she had none. He wrote her letters but they were destroyed. Many a false report concerning him was conjured up and poured into her ears by her unfeeling mistress, who would come into the kitchen, light her pipe and sit leisurely down to rehearse to my mother what she had heard about "James," every word of it the product of her own fertile imagination, and told purely for the purpose of making mother miserable. So when the mistress appeared at the door of the hut, and lighting her pipe, sat down for one of her cheerful (?) interviews, mother

usually knew that some big story was to
follow. She would preface her remarks
by saying, "Well, I heard from James today. The 'Yankees' have got him." And
then would follow some horrible recital
of how the "Yankees" had him chained to
an anvil block and were starving him to
death, or something else equally consol-
ing. At such times mother would calmly
answer, "Oh, well, he is as well off there
as he would be here."

The slave-holders who had sent their
slaves to Georgia to prevent the "Yankees" getting them now began to think
that the war was about over, as every-
thing seemed to calm down; and Mr.
Suggs said with the others, "Well, we can
bring our niggers back now, the d—d
Yankees have left Corinth." The general
feeling was that of safety, and there was
little fear that the Union army would
again bother them. So the exiled slaves
were sent for, and with them came moth-

er's children, Ellen and Frank. They had been abused and sadly neglected, but in answer to prayer, they were restored to their mother.

But the calm in which they had trusted was the calm of death. It was the lull before the bursting of the thunderbolt. The "Yankees" returned in greater numbers than ever, and in less than two months peace was proclaimed. Mother could see so clearly the hand of God in the restoration of her children in His own appointed time and manner; as had they been left in Georgia until the close of the war, it is very doubtful, humanly speaking, as to whether she would ever have seen them again. And for this reason: So long as the slaves were considered *property,* each owner naturally looked after his own belongings and kept them together. After the slaves were freed, however, no one cared what became of them. And so it was at the close of the

war, that many families were separated
and were never reunited. My mother had
eight brothers and sisters, and cannot tell
where one of them is today. That she
ever got back her children was due to
God's own arrangement and overruling.

But this curse of African slavery is
done away. Thank God! Parents and
children, husbands and wives, are no
longer torn from each other and sold as
cattle to enrich their master. We have one
Master, even God. We have lived to see
the day when "all men are born free and
equal," and this despite of race or color.
The blot of African slavery has been wiped out from our fair land with the life-
blood of her brave sons. But there still
exists in our very midst, another, and
even more cruel slavery, which is holding
men soul and body in the most abject
bondage. It is the slavery of Intemper-
ance. The white man's slave could love
and serve the Lord and in the end get to

heaven. The Drink Demon's slave is held with an ever tightening grip in life, and is ruined, body and soul, in death. Shall we see the curse of strong drink wiped out even as we have seen the curse of slavery? Shall we have an Emancipation Proclamation for the defenceless millions over whom drink is now tyranizing? I appeal to you who are voters. Shall we?

After mother was set free, she left her old master and went to work out. Ellen and Frank were old enough to do a little; so they were put out to service too. One day there came a letter to mother. In it was a lock of father's hair. She knew the hair and the handwriting, and knew it was no fraud. This letter told her to prepare to come north with Captain Newton. Could it be possible that so much of good was in store for her? Yes, it was really true. Mr. Newton had gone to Georgia and would be back again in a month after her and the children. But he being a

FOUR GENERATIONS.

Mrs. Siggs, Daughter, Grandson and Great-Granddaughter.

Union man, it was dangerous for him to stay long in the south. So he had to hurry back and come for mother sooner than he expected. But she left all and went with him, and the long-divided family were now at last happily reunited.

Of these four children born in slavery, Ellen is the only one now surviving, Lucinda died with typhoid fever at the age of eight. Calvin took quick consumption from exposure in Michigan, and died at the age of nineteen. Franklin grew to manhood and was married. Three months after his marriage, he was drowned in a lake near Elgin, Illinois. Ellen, the eldest child, now Mrs. Ellen Thompson, lived in Elgin until two years ago, since which time she has lived near Omaha, Nebraska.

After the days of slavery, while my parents were living in Bureau county, Illinois, there were born to them four daughters, Sarah Matilda, Katharine Isabel,

Lenora Ethridge, and the writer, Eliza Gertrude, all of whom are still living.

During my father's last illness he often spoke to mother about temporal needs, and would always end by saying, "The Lord will provide." And truly He has. Mother in her declining years has a comfortable home, free from debt, near the church, where she delights to attend. She is always found in her place in the house of God unless prevented by illness. And although getting along in years, she is seldom ill. She gets a pension and with this gets along nicely. Verily, the willing and obedient shall eat the good of the land.

Father Take My Hand.

The way is dark, my Father, cloud on cloud
Is gathering thickly o'er my head, and loud
The thunders roar above me. See, I stand
Like one bewildered: Father, take my hand,
    And through the gloom
    Lead safely home
      Thy child!

The day goes fast, my Father, and the night
Is dawning darkly down. My faithless sight
Sees ghostly visions. Fears, a spectral band,
Encompass me, O, Father, take my hand,
    And from the night,
    Lead up to light
      Thy child!

The way is long, my Father! and my soul
Longs for the rest and quiet of the goal;
While yet I journey through this weary land,
Keep me from wandering. Father, take my hand;
    Quickly and straight,
    Lead to heaven's gate
      Thy child!

The path is rough, my Father! Many a thorn
Has pierced me; and my weary feet, all torn
And bleeding, mark the way. Yet thy command
Bids me press forward. Father, take my hand;
  Then safe and blest,
  Lead up to rest
   Thy child!

The throng is great, my Father! Many a doubt
And fear and danger compass me about;
And foes oppress me sore. I cannot stand
Or go alone. O, Father! take my hand,
  And through the throng
  Lead safe along
   Thy child!

The cross is heavy, Father! I have borne
It long, and still do bear it. Let my worn
And fainting spirit rise to that blest land
Where crowns are given. Father, take my hand;
  And reaching down,
  Lead to the crown
   Thy child!

      —Henry N. Cobb.

The Gracious Answer.

The way is dark, my child! but leads to light.
I would not always have thee walk by sight.
My dealings now thou canst not understand.
I meant it so; but I will take thy hand,
      And through the gloom,
      Lead safely home
        My child!

The day goes fast, my child! But is the night
Darker to me than day? In me is light!
Keep close to me and every spectral band
Of fears shall vanish. I will take thy hand,
      And through the night
      Lead up to light
        My child!

The way is long, my child! But it shall be
Not one step longer than is best for thee;
And thou shalt know, at last, when thou shalt
    stand
Safe at the goal, how I did take thy hand.
      And quick and straight,
      Lead to heaven's gate
        My child!

The path is rough, my child! But oh! how sweet
Will be the rest, for weary pilgrims meet,
When thou shalt reach the borders of that land
To which I lead thee, as I take thy hand;
      And safe and blest
      With me shall rest,
        My child!

The throng is great, my child! But at thy side
Thy Father walks; then be not terrified,
For I am with thee; will thy foes command
To let thee freely pass; will take thy hand,
      And through the throng
      Lead safe along,
        My child!

                       —Henry N. Cobb.

Sketch of Eliza.

"My cage confines me round;
  Abroad I cannot fly;
But though my wing is closely bound,
  My heart's at liberty.
My prison walls cannot control
The flight, the freedom, of the soul."
                    —Madame Guyon.

On the 11th day of December, 1876, near Providence, Bureau county, Illinois, the subject of this sketch was born. I seemed to be a healthy baby, and for a short time grew as other children. But at four weeks old, my bones began to snap and break. One day I cried all day, and my mother wondered what could be the matter. She found out that one of my limbs was broken. In time it healed, and lo an arm broke. This had no more than recovered when the other arm broke. And thus my bones would break, one after another, for six long years. Whenever

I was moved, it caused me great suffering. My bones being very soft and tender, just the least thing would cause them to break. One day my little sister Lenora, two years older, was showing me how some people shook hands at meeting. As she shook my hand to show me, my arm broke.

I knew nothing of the pleasures of childhood. I could not play as other children, but had to sit still in the house and look out at the other children; and part of the time was not even able to sit up. I was doctored but without any apparent benefit. The doctors in those days did not seem to understand my case. But the doctors now say it was an extreme case of the rickets, such as they have read about but have very rarely seen. My mother prayed for the Lord to take me out of my intense suffering. There was not a thought that I could live. My burial clothes were made, and everybody expected that they would shortly be needed. But

God saw fit to let me live. His thoughts
are not our thoughts, neither are His ways
our ways. If any one had said to my
mother that I should live to be twenty-
eight years old, she would have said it
was out of the question. I stopped grow-
ing. For years my weight was only
twenty-four or twenty-five pouns; but in
later years I have gained some in weight,
though not in height. My weight at the
present time is about fifty pounds and my
height about thirty-three inches. I ride
in a baby carriage or go-cart, and am
often taken for a baby and spoken to as
such.

As I go about, being so small for my
age, I am quite a curiosity to strangers.
I have often been amused when people
would crowd around me and ask mother
or Sister Katie questions about me, such
as, "Can she talk?" "Is she smart?" "How
old is the baby?" 'Has she got feet?"
"Can she use her hands?" "Oh what a

big baby!" One lady on the train, not long ago, came up to me and began to talk baby talk. "Hello, sir! Hello, sir! Boo!" This was indeed amusing to me. It drew the attention of every one in the car. Of course, the baby did not respond in the way she expected, she supposing it would laugh and crow. When I was explained to her she was somewhat taken back.

I am often asked if I do not get tired sitting all the time. Of course, I know nothing else only sit, as I never walked a step in my life. I know it must be grand to be able to walk, but I know nothing from experience, of the pleasures of walking. Some day, I expect to walk the streets of the New Jerusalem just as well as those who now have the full use of their feet; and that will be exceedingly grand.

If I had been strong and healthy like other children and young people, perhaps

I should not have known the Lord. I
might now have been running after the
pleasures of the world. I can't remember when I first began to pray. One day
while lying on the bed in my room alone,
the Lord came to me. I wanted to be a
Christian and know that I was saved.
While praying for this the Lord heard my
prayer and blessed my soul. I was not at
that time, more than five years old, and I
have served the Lord ever since. I am
thankful I have been preserved and kept
from the wickedness of the world.

The Lord is so good to me. He often
comes to my heart with such refreshing
peace. He melts my heart so that it is
easy to pray. I say, Oh, Lord, just help
me to pray and prevail with Thee for
others." This world is full of suffering
humanity. There are many in distress,
running after the world, seeking peace
and finding none. The Lord helps me to
pray for such. I cannot help longing to

be in the active work of the Lord, helping
to rescue poor lost souls, and those who
are blinded in sin. But perhaps God can
get more glory out of me as an invalid
than He could if I were well. He can
help me to pray for those who are strong
and able to work in His vineyard. I know
there is nothing accomplished for God
without earnest prayer. So I am content
to fill my little corner and be what God
wants me to be. I say from my heart,
"Thy will be done in earth as it is in
heaven."

I was necessarily deprived, to a great
extent of school privileges. My sisters
taught me my letters and how to spell. I
loved to learn. After we moved to Kansas, my sister Sarah taught school near a
place called Big Bend, but afterward
named Speed. There was no schoolhouse
in the neighborhood, so she taught in one
room of our house. This was a large
room and served quite well for the pur-

pose. This gave me a chance to go to school at home. I was greatly delighted; and as it did not hurt me to sit in school, I was allowed to study as much as I liked.

In time, my sisters went away from home to Orleans, Nebraska, to attend school at the Seminary. Then my father moved to Orleans to give them the benefit of the school. We settled close to the seminary to be handy to school and church; but still no one thought it possible for me to attend school, until in 1889, when my dear friend, Emma H. Hillmon, now Mrs. Emma H. Haviland, was Principal of the Seminary. God put it into her heart to give me a chance to go to school. She came to see my mother and offered to give me free tuition in the seminary, and urged mother to send me. So every day I was wheeled to school in my invalid chair, which friends on the Sappa had kindly donated me; and was carried up the steps to the school room by mother or Katie, and placed at my desk, where I sat until lessons were over and they came for me at noon and night. My bones did not break any more. I was *comparatively* healthy, and nothing prevented my attending school. I was now fairly started in school and eager to learn. The following year the seminary closed; but the next year, under Rev. C. E. Harroun, Jr., the way was again open for me to attend school, and I gladly embraced the opportunity.

Ever since I was old enough to know anything about the awful curse of strong drink, I have been greatly interested in temperance work, and have felt like lifting my voice in this grand cause whenever opportunity presented. I have many times felt the blessing of God in singing temperance songs or in speaking temperance recitations. While in school at Orleans several young people were carefully trained by Sister Emma Hillmon on the Demorest Medal temperance recitations. These were spoken from time to time in the Seminary chapel before large audiences. Judges were appointed who were to observe critically every word and gesture and award the medal to the best speaker. It was in one of these contests that I won the silver medal which I have on in my picture, shown on another page. This medal I could never wear for pride or show, but only on special occasions to show my interest in the temperance cause and my relation to it.

Rev. J. Adams, now living at Greenville, Illinois, but at that time pastor at Orleans, sometimes gave temperance lectures around at county schoolhouses. At such times he would often take with him some of the students from the seminary to sing, and I was sometimes called upon to speak or sing in these meetings.

Of later years my thoughts and attention have been called more particularly to foreign missionary work. When my dear friend, Miss Hillmon, left Orleans, on her way to Africa, my heart was stirred. I longed to go too and work for the elevation and salvation of my own race. All the years she was in Africa I was in close correspondence with her, and felt that in spirit, if not in bodily presence, I was by her side. Since, I have had the pleasure of meeting several different missionaries from Africa, India, and China, and have come to feel a deep interest in every heathen land. Since I can never go myself to carry the Gospel to the heathen, I esteem it a great privilege to help hold the ropes in this country, and to pray for and encourage those who go.

As I look back over my past life, and remember how good the Lord has been to me through all my sufferings, I am made to wonder. But if He can get any glory

ELIZA SUGGS AND FOUR SISTERS, MRS. L. E. SELBY, MISS K. I. SUGGS, MRS. S. M. WILLIAMS, MRS. S. E. THOMPSON.

out of my life I shall be satisfied. There
have been persons who would say to my
mother, "Why don't you take her to the
show or museum? That wouldn't be any
harm and you could make your living easily." Others would say, "There is
a fortune in that girl." Quite recently a
gentleman said to my niece, as he saw me
for the first time, "There is ready money."

But, dear reader, God did not create
me for this purpose. He created me for
His glory, and if I can be a help to any
one, and if God can get glory to His name
out of my life, amen! To this end shall I
live. It has never been a temptation to
me to want to go with a show or to be in
a museum for money making purposes.
I once went to a museum in Chicago just
to see and learn. I was asked by one there
why I did not speak to the manager and
get a place in the museum, and make lots
of money. Oh, no! Such places are not
for me. God wants me to live for Him,

and I could not do it there. I must keep separated from the world. "Wherefore come out from among them and be ye separate, saith the Lord, and touch not the unclean thing; and I will receive you; and will be a father unto you, and ye shall be my sons and daughters, saith the Lord Almighty." The love of God in my heart keeps me from wanting to do the things that God disapproves and I love to do the things that He approves.

Some wonder how I can be happy in my condition. It is the sunlight of God in my soul that makes me happy. It would be hard to live without the Lord. I get much pleasure from the reading of good books. I enjoy looking at the beautiful things in nature and in art. I love to listen to the singing of the birds and to sweet music. In fact many pleasures come to me through the five senses, of which I have full use. Then too, I have good use of my hands and can work and earn a little. And of the little I earn, the Lord gets the tenth. That is His. I am so thankful that the Lord enables me to work in this way. For if I could not use my hands, or if I could not read, time would drag heavily, and life would become very monotonous. The work I do is knitting, crocheting, fancy work, and making horse hair watch chains. The Lord always provides a way for His children.

And then I am blessed in having a host of friends. Every one is so good to me, and seeks to make my life pleasant and cheerful. I have many pleasant hours with the teachers and students of the Orleans Seminary. I can never forget them. They have been such a help to me.

Another blessing I enjoy is a comfortable home, just a few rods from the seminary, where I attend Sunday School and church. Our home is a home where the Lord has come to dwell. Our family is small now. A part have crossed over the

river.   There are five girls left, myself
and four sisters, three of whom are married.   Our family now at home consists of
mother, myself, and Sister Katie, my
faithful attendant.   I am thankful to God
that He has spared to me my dear mother
and sister, who have cared for me so kindly and tenderly all these years.   In all
of my helplessness, and now more espec-
ially in mother's old age and failing
health, Katie has been and is today our
cheerful and faithful standby.   She has
surely had abundant opportunities for
the exercise of patience.   Of her it shall
be said, "She hath done what she could."
"Inasmuch as ye have done it unto one of
the least of these my brethren, ye have
done it unto me."

Perfect Through Suffering.

God never would send you the darkness
  If He felt you could bear the light;
But you would not cling to His guiding hand
  If the way were always bright;
And you would not care to walk by faith,
  Could you always walk by sight.

'Tis true He has many an anguish,
  For our sorrowful hearts to bear;
And many a cruel thorn-crown
  For your tired head to wear;
He knows how few would reach heav'n at all
  If pain did not guide them there.

So He sends you the blinding darkness,
  And the furnace of seven-fold heat;
'Tis the only way,, believe me,
  To keep you close to His feet,
For 'tis always so easy to wander
  . When our lives are glad and sweet.

Then nestle your hand in your Father's,
  And sing, if you can, as you go;
Your song may cheer somo one behind you
  Whose courage is sinking low,
And, well, if your lips do quiver
  God will love you better so.

                    —Sel.

Incidents of Slavery.

The time of slavery were troublous times, to those who felt its crushing power. Life, liberty, and the pursuit of happiness, have been defined as the inalienable rights of every human being. To have an existence as a human being, and yet to be held under such bondage as deprives one of all human rights,—such an existence must ever be a misery. With no right to have property, family, or even a name of his own apart from that of his master, to the slave, the pursuit of happiness was a terribly disappointing one. Yet in just such a condition of thralldom were held four millions of Africa's sons and daughters on American soil, until at one stroke by the Emancipation Proclamation, the shackles were riven, and these millions of lowly creatures were human beings in reality as well as in name.

The following incidents of slave life, with many others like them, have been related by my mother as having come under her own observation. There was a man in Mississippi by the name of Gregory, who was very cruel to his slaves; so much so, that they would run away from him whenever they got a chance. Rarely, however, did one succeed in escaping, for the blood-hounds were at once on their track. Mngled and bleeding, they were caught and brought back, and as a punishment for running away, they were required to work on the Sabbath day to make up their lost time. Mr. Gregory went out one Sabbath to oversee the delinquents in some wood-chopping. A tree, in falling, accidentally lodged in another tree. This angered the master, and in no very amiable mood, he set to work to help pull it down, when by some mismanagement, it fell on him and killed him in-

stantly.   This would seem a just judg-
ment for his unrighteousness.

The marriage ceremony for slaves had
in it a clause requiring them to cleave to
each other 'until distance should them
part'; meaning until their master sold
them apart.   One day we heard a terrible
screaming in the road which passed our
house, and on going out to see what the
trouble was about, there was poor Amy
Griffin, crying and wringing her hands in
awful agony, as she was hurried along
the road between two strange men.   "Oh
my poor husband! I shall never see you
any more—never any more!"   She had
been sold away from her husband, and
they were taking her hundreds of miles
away.

One master who lived near us had large
cotton fields and about one hundred
slaves.   Each one was required to pick a
certain amount of cotton daily.   The
amount varied somewhat with different

individuals, and was from fifty to one hundred pounds, according to the age and strength of the picker. No allowance was made for temporary illness or indisposition on the part of any slave. Each was expected, invariably, to measure up to his apportionment. At the end of the day, every basket was weighed by a white man. Any shortage in weight was punished by a terrible beating with a large ox-hide whip. Very often would be heard the screams of poor slaves who had failed to pick their full quota.

After the day's work was over, the slaves had dealt out to them some corn meal and fat bacon, which each had to prepare for himself in his own cabin. They must prepare at night enough for the next day. This was carried to the field and eaten cold, so there should be no loss of time from their work.

All the masters were not like this, however. I had a good, kind master. I was

one of the fortunate ones. I was never
abused like this; but my poor mother did
not have a square inch of smooth skin on
her back. The lash had cut deep gashes
which left ugly scars and ridges.

I have seen my poor people bought up
by hundreds, and word sent out that "a
drove of niggers" was to be in town on a
certain day. The poor things would be
lined up in rows, men, women, and children; and one after another they were
sold, from an auction block to the highest
bidder. Miserable, contemptible white
men would examine that human property,
much as you would examine a horse, even
thrusting open jaws to examine the teeth,
and feeling the muscles of arm or body.
I have seen them pass their rough hands
over the arms, neck, and bust of women
and girls, and ask such questions as were
degrading in the extreme; and yet the
poor creatures could not help themselves

—no, not though every instinct of decency or modesty was outraged.

I have seen the little baby taken from its mother's breast and sold hundreds of miles away, never to be seen or heard of again. A mother who lived near us had a little son sold away from her at about two years of age, and was never able to get any trace of him afterward, until very unexpectedly, and by the merest accident, she discovered her lost son. After the war was over and slaves were free, she met and loved a man and was finally married to him. One day she observed a peculiar scar on his head, and told him of her little son who had a similar scar caused by a kick from a horse when he was a baby. They began to investigate, and found that he was her long lost boy. She had married her own child!

My people were, many of them, God-fearing, and took advantage of every chance they had to meet together and

serve the Lord. They would sometimes
be permitted to occupy the back seats of
the white man's church. But when the
white people came in sufficient numbers
to fill the church, the slaves were ordered
out of doors. They had no choice as to
what church they should attend, but were
obliged to attend the same church as their
master. The sacrament was administered
to them separately.

Among themselves they sometimes had
powerful meetings, and would get saved
and blest and feel the joys of another
world. This would cause them to forget,
for the time being, their miseries in this.
Faith would catch a gleam of the day
when they should burst their shackles and
go free. For this they sighed and cried
and prayed. And there came a day, thank
God, when the groans and cries of the op-
pressed reached the ears of the Heavenly
Father; and though He delayed a while,

yet He did come and show His power, and His colored children are free today. And for this I desire to give Him all the glory.

The Octoroon.

1. In the palmy days of slavery,
    A score of years ago,
   A pretty, dark-skinned Octoroon
    Was singing soft and low
   A song to please her baby
    As in her arms it lay,
   A dainty, dimpled, fair-haired boy—
    A twelve-month old that day.

2. Strange home for child or mother!
    For her quick ear often heard,
   'Mid the clink of dice and glasses,
    Many a loud and angry word.
   For her Phillip was a gambler;
    But she never dreamed or thought
   Of any shame or sorrow
    For the wrongs he might have wrought.

3. "He plays 'seven-up' 'till midnight,"
    She often laughing told,
   "And then, like other gentlemen,
    Comes home and counts his gold."

4. So she was always happy,
    Singing French songs, sweet and wild,

With a voice as full of music
  As the laughing of a child.
But, the midnight, she was waiting
  For his footstep on the stair,
Came a sound of measured meaning
  Throbbing on the silent air!

5. Came a sound of troubled voices,
      Filling all her soul with dread—
    Comrads, bearing up a burden,
      Cold and lifeless! Phil was dead!
    Like a sudden blow, it smote her
      With a desolate sense of grief,
    But no faintness came to shield her,
      And no tears to bring relief.

6. Oh, to escape the heart-ache,
      And the dumb, bewildering pain.
    How gladly would she fall asleep
      And never wake again!
    Yet, she watched with heart near breaking
      As they bore his form away;
    Then she listened to the prosing
      Of two lawyers, old and gray.

7. As they talked of debts of honor,
      Of the house, and horses fine,
    Of, plate, perhaps and jewels;
      Of furniture and wine;

Then! Ah! Then, what was the meaning
  Of the words they muttered o'er?
As they said: "The wench and baby
  Ought to bring a thousand more!"

8. Quickened ears and comprehension
      Caught each careless tone and word;
    Knew too well the tricks of trade
      To doubt the fearful truth she heard.
    But when they so roughly told her:
      "There will be a sale tomorrow!"
    Her voice broke forth in piteous wail
      Of bitterness and sorrow:—

9. "Oh, I know Phil never meant
      For me and baby to be sold!
    Why, I'se been his little woman
      Since I'se only twelve years old!
    He won me from the Captin,
      Playing 'seven-up' one night,
    And he's told me more'n a thousand times
      He's sure to make it right.

10. The Captin was my father,
      Captin Winslow, of Bellair,
    And you can't sell me and baby—
      O you can't! You never dare!"
    And those men, so used to suffering,
      And callous as they were,

ELIZA SUGGS. AGE 16.

Looked in each other's faces
And paused to pity her.

11. But "many a case was just as bad,
       And some perhaps were worse;
   They could do nothing, anyhow,
       The law must take its course."
   The broken hearted mother
       Tried in vain to sleep that night,
   Her busy brain would conjure up
       Some possible means of flight.

12. Well she knew she was a prisoner,
       That the house was thronged with men;
   Knew, too, that for years this place
       Had been a noted gambler's den,
   And a long, low vaulted chamber
       Ran beneath the basement floor,
   Opening far beyond detection,
       In a heavy, hidden door.

13. She shuddered with a vision
       Of the bloodhounds on her track,
   As she thought deadly certain
       They would be to bring her back!

14. O, she could not, could not bear it!
       She would kill herself and him!
   Then, across her 'wildered memory
       Stole a vision faint and dim,

Of some reverent childish teaching,
  Prayer to God, and faith and fear—
"Lead us not into temptation!"
  Was He listening? Did He hear?

15. Then she thought of old Aunt Dinah,
      Who had taught her thus to pray,
    Living free in Oppoloosa,
      Half a score of miles away.

16. And at last, she rose, determined
      That the danger should be braved;
    Though her life might pay the forfeit,
      Little Phillip should be saved!
    So she wrapped her sleeping treasure
      In a mantle dark and thin,
    Tied a gaudy-hued bandana
      'Neath her smoothly-rounded chin,

17. Planned her flight to escape detection,
      And removing every trace,
    With a subtle, stealthy movement
      Of a leopard, left the place.
    And she paused not in the journey,—
      Life or death still lay before!
    'Till she struggled, worn and weary,
      To Aunt Dinah's cabin door.

18. Hush! a voice of prayer and pleading
     On the midnight calm is heard:—
   "Teach us, Lord, through all our blindness
     To believe Thy precious word.
   Help us when our hearts are heavy;
     Guide us when we go astray;
   Lead us in the paths we know not,
     Nearer to Thee, day by day."

19. With her spirit vision opened
     By some unseen inner sight,
   Old Aunt Dinah had arisen
     And was praying in the night.
   In her strong, black arms she gathered
     Weary mother, wondering child;
   And she listened to their story
     Full of anguish, fierce and wild.

20. Knowing well she could not save them,
     That her love though strong and bright,
   Was as chaff before the whirlwind
     Of the white man's power and might.
   "I would give my poor old heart's blood,
     Every drop for yours and you,
   If I could but keep you, honey,
     From this path you'r walking through.

21. But, I've seen it all too often;
     They will hunt you if you hide,

They will catch you if you'r fleeing,
  They will take you from my side;
And they'll take your baby from you,
  Stop! De Lord's own voice I hear;
Will you trust your precious darling
  To my care and leave him here?

22. "I will keep him from all danger;
  Hide him where no eye can see;
And 'twill be a comfort deary,
  If you always know he's free.
Don't look so; give me the baby;
  Yes, I know how hard it is,
But we do the Father's bidding,
  Not in our way, but in His.

23. "I will pray for you tomorrow;
  Now the moon is going down,
You must take my little donkey,
  Child, and hurry back to town.
Ride him just as far's you dare to,
  Then tie up the bridle rein,
Turn his head, he's done sartain
  To come right straight home again!"

24. When next morning she was summoned
  From her room, she walked alone;
Though her fierce, brown eyes burned darkly,
  They were tearless, dry as stone.

And the lawyers and the keepers
  Looked at her and shrank away,
'Minded by her wondrous beauty
  Of a tigress turned at bay.

25. But a query ran among them,—
  Of the baby—where was he?
'Till she heard their words and answered
  Very calmly—"He is free!"
"Free! The house was strongly guarded,
  Every window, every door;
They had seen both child and mother
  Safely caged the night before!

26. "Not a living thing had ventured
  O'er the threshold that they knew;
And the hounds with hungry voices
  Bayed outside the whole night through."
Instant search sufficed to show them
  That the baby was not there;
Not a hint, or trace, or sign
  Could they discover anywhere.

27. Then, with threatening look and gesture
  To the mother they returned,
But she said in words triumphant,
  While her eyes more brightly burned:—

28. "Strike me! Minions! I expect it!
  Scourge me! burn me! beat or kill!

But it will not help you find him,
  He is Free! my darling Phil!
Think you, I would fear to hide him
  In the darkness of the grave?
Ah, my baby's father's baby
Was not born to be a slave!"

29. So, with furtive eyes they watched her,
       Talking low 'mid fear and fright,
     Half afraid 'mid their bravado,
       She would vanish from their sight.
     But she stood as stands the martyr,
       When his last frail hope dies out,
     And the murmuring sea of voices
       Rises to an angry shout.

30. And she thought not of her beauty
       As her heart beat fast and faster,
     Gazing on those stranger faces,
       Wondering which would be her master.
     But, the horrid truth awoke her,—
       "Going, going, gone!" It told
     That beyond all hope or dreaming,
       She was sold,—to slavery sold!

31. Then, as if the soul within her
       Larger grew with pain and strife,
     Or, as if some marble statue
       Started forth, a thing of life,

Turned she, with the footsteps silent
  As a specter of the dead,
From their midst she swiftly fled,
  Ere a hand could lift to stay her.

32. On—to where the lofty margin
    Overlooked the river's flood,
  There she paused and turned in triumph
    As upon its brink she stood:
  "Cowards! Do you dare to follow
    To your gulf, to find your slave?
  Think you that I fear to render
    Back to God the life He gave.

33. Let him in his righteous Judgement
    Weigh the guilt 'twixt you and me;
  Let him guard my boy and keep him
    When his mother, too, is free!
  Back! you have no power to stay me!
    Stop! I would not hear you lie,
  Back! I laugh at you, my masters!
    Free I ..ve! and free I die!"

34. Turning with a look of triumph
    And a smile of proud disdain,
  Sprang she forth into the river,
    Sank, and rose—and sank again.
  Onward swept the mighty river
    On its journey to the sea;
  But the mother's woes were ended—
    Child and mother both were free.
                        —Selected.

Pauline the Reaper.

"A beautiful time for the harvest"
  Said Pauline, the reaper, one day;
My sheaves shall be many and golden
  When the Master cometh this way;
My place is where grain is the ripest,
  And my hands are young and strong;
Nor care I for heat or (for) labor
  As I sing the reaper's song.
Gathering, gathering for the King,
Hands may grow weary but glad hearts sing,
    "Till he comes."

"Pauline,"—'twas the voice of the Master,
  And she paused in her happy haste,
Where for the want of a skilful reaper
  Ripe grain was going to waste.
Pauline, "Leave there thy sheaf unbinded,
  And now come aside with me"
Was the Master's word of greeting
  "I, something would say to thee."
And she heard the happy ringing
Of the reapers in their singing
    "Till He comes."

"Wait here and help on the harvest,"
  Was the Master's strange command,
As she reached a lonely corner
  And folded her eager hands.
She waited in painful silence
  Waited with weary heart;
For how could she help the reapers
  If she did not do her part.
Afar she could hear them calling
  "Thy beautiful grain is falling,
Pauline, Pauline, art thou hiding;
Thou wilt have nothing but chiding,
    When He comes."

Her heart was heavy with sorrow,
  And desolate was the cry,
Oh, why, when I love my Master
  Am I like a weed thrown by?
I left the world and its treasures
  Nor heeded a moment its cost
To take my place with the reapers,
  Now all my talents are lost.
Nevermore will I be singing
Where the ripest grain is springing
    When He comes."

"Pauline," 'twas the voice of the Master,
  "The harvest is mine, not thine
If waiting gives me best service

Surely thou needst not repine,
Another has taken thy sickle;
 It only is left to thee
To see in this lone hidden corner
 What work can be done for me.
There can be no place so dreary,
 There can be no place so weary,
But that all can help in bringing
Golden sheaves with happy singing,
  Till I come."

So she smiled and gave a welcome
 To pain which would be her guest;
And patience and sweet submission
 Came soon with their helpful rest,
With their help in her shadowed corner,
 Like stars through the gathering gloom,
There sprang for Pauline fairest flowers
 That filled every spot with bloom.
Then the Master came so often,
 It was caled a holy place
And the weary reapers lingered
 For more love and lowly grace;
And they went their own way singing
"We shall all be ripe grain bringing
  Till He comes."

"Thou canst plan for the busy workers"
 Pauline heard the Master say!

And she joyfully took the message
  And said when one passed her way
"Take flowers to the darkened prisons,
  And glooms to the bed of pain
And blossoms to the weary mother
  Thy labor will not be vain"
They heeded her gentle bidding
  And fragrance went everywhere,
While tired eyes were lifted upward
  And sad hearts were saved despair.
In her room came back the echo
  Of the reapers in their singing
    "Till He comes."

"'Tis time the sheaves were garnered"
  Said the Master when eve had come
And the reapers in the gloaming
  Were singing their harvest home.
Then Pauline observed in wonder
  As they entered the sunset gate
Her name on sheaves rich and golden
  That were gathered early and late.
And the Master smiled approval
  And said as she meekly came,
"Thine is the crown of the toilers
  That were garnered for me in thy name"
And the bells of heaven were ringing
While the angel choir was singing
    "He has come."   —Selected.

The Holy Guest.

by Eliza Suggs.

O, the blessed Holy One,
Hath come within my heart to dwell,
And the good that He has done
My tongue can never tell.

He took away my stony heart,
And put a heart of flesh therein.
And now O sin thou hast no part
But Jesus dwells within.

He has bidden sin depart,
And has entered my heart's door
Saying, "Now my child thou art,
Go, and sin no more."

The Drunkard's Wife.

by Eliza Suggs.

Here sits a dear old lady
  In her rustic chair,
Sunbeams gently falling
  On her snow-white hair.
There is a sad, sad story,
  Written on her face
Sorrow and woe, long, long ago,
  Have left the sad lines you trace.

Chorus:
        She had a drunken husband!
          After all these years,
        Golden hair is silver now,
          Dim those eyes with tears.
        She had a drunken husband
          Waiting him to reform.
        He went away one bitter cold day
          He now fills a drunkard's grave.

Far, far away McDonald
  Went in revelry.
"Stay, I pray you husband,
  Do not go away.
That is the road to ruin,
  That is the road to sin.
Says the word of God, in Heaven above,
  No drunkard shall enter in.

"Just one glass, McDonald,"
Said his comrades dear.
"Just this once to please us
  A social glass of beer."
"Just this once to please you
  I take my first glass now.
I'll take no more, dear wife, I'm sure,
  I make to you this vow."

That was his first step downward;
  On and on he went.
Powerful grew the habit
  Downward he was bent,—
Drank 'till he raved in madness,
  Then came the fatal day
With a curse and stare and clutching
      his hair,
  His soul then passed away.

When the sad tidings reached her
  She fell, they thought her dead,
Then there came a doctor,
  "A broken heart," he said.
That's why she's sad and lonely,
  Waiting for him in vain;
He went away one bitter cold day,
  And never returned again.

The Death of the Old Year.

by Eliza Suggs.

Tick tock, tick tock, time is flying
Tick tock, tick tock, the old year is dying
Soon the Old Year will be gone
Soon the New Year will be on
So the time is flying
Tick tock, tick tock.

Tick tock, tick tock, time is flitting
Tick tock, tick tock, no time for fretting
But let us always keep in view
Our days on earth are few
And there's lots of work to do
Tick tock, tick tock.

Tick tock, tick tock, the clock is striking
Tick tock, tick tock just while I'm writing
Another hour has swiftly gone
The Old Year is nearly gone.
Oh, how the time is hastening on,
Tick tock, tick tock.

Tick tock, tick tock, time is going
Tick tock, tick tock, what are we doing?

We must labor hard to find
Souls for God, and bear in mind
We'll not always have this time.
Tick tock, tick tock.

Tick tock, tick tock, sixty minutes more
Tick tock, tick tock, the Old year will be o'er
Twelve oclock has now rolled round
Old Year has entirely gone
Happy New Year now has come
Tick tock, tick tock.

Tick tock, tick tock, soon time will be no more
Tick tock, tick tock, then all will be o'er
Let us labor hard this year
Working for the Lord with fear
Eternity is drawing near,
Tick tock, tick tock.

CPSIA information can be obtained
at www.ICGtesting.com
Printed in the USA
LVHW021958110221
679098LV00041B/1035